Mindful
Moments

Michelle Neely Stowe

Michelle Neely Stowe
12-01-2018

Library of Congress Control Number:
2018956250

ISBN-13: 978-0692135280
ISBN-10: 0692135286

Cover design by Shannon Georger-Clifford
SG-GRAPHIX.COM

DEDICATION

This book is dedicated to every woman who has at some point in her life needed an extra word of encouragement but instead gave a word of encouragement; who has at some point in her life felt fearful about pursuing her dreams but persevered; who has at some point in her life looked at the obstacles she was facing and questioned if she had enough strength to endure but won the battle anyway. To every woman who is willing to commit to her destiny and guide another woman along life's journey, this book is for you.

ACKNOWLEDGEMENTS

I would like to give honor to my Lord and Savior, Jesus Christ, Who is the Alpha and Omega of my life, for without Him I realize nothing would be possible, but with Him all things are possible.

With my heart overflowing with love, I acknowledge my children, Noah Stowe and Savannah Stowe. In so many ways, you two are a source of strength and encouragement for me. Thank you both for always believing in your momma's dreams.

I would like to recognize my family members. I will not list you by name for the fear of omitting someone. However, for those of you who have stood by me in my greatest moments and in my not-so-notable moments, those who have encouraged me when it appeared that all my chips were down, and to those who look at me and say, "We will just go with your flow," I say thank you for your support.

To my closest friends, whom I will not list by name, but you will recognize your role, I say thank you. Thank you for listening to all my entrepreneurial dreams, for challenging me to keep moving forward, and for taking my phone calls no matter what time my vision appeared and I needed to share it. Thank you for just being there, not because you had to but because you chose to.

To my Best Friend on a very special level, you were the first one with whom I shared my vision for my business and my books. I thank you for everything. Thank you for never letting me settle. Thank you for not being afraid to challenge me. Thank you because no matter what level of success I achieve, you always seem to see the next level of success on the inside of me. Most importantly, thank you for not conforming to my world but challenging me to create the world that I envisioned.

To my editor, Monica Y. Dennis, and the staff at On-Call Editing, I appreciate your commitment, effort, and time. Monica, thank you for the numerous phone calls and the unlimited amount of guidance and direction.

INTRODUCTION

As women, we are often so busy and have so much going on — family, work, school, friends, and activities. We do not always take the time to establish a point of focus for ourselves for the day or for the moment. But I have learned when I do establish my focal point at the beginning of my day, I am more aware of the empowerment inside me to achieve the goal.

These daily quotes are intended to give you inspiration, encouragement, empowerment, moments of self-reflection, moments of re-dedication, and opportunities for growth. These quotes are in no way intended to re-place daily time in God's Word but are intended to help every woman search within her soul to align her focus for the day with God's Word.

As women, we can all agree that in so many ways, we are as different as can be. Some of us are mothers, some of us are not. Some of us are homemakers and some of us are active businesswomen, while some of us are both. Some of us have loving and supportive families, while some of us are pursuing our dreams on our own. Some of us have a lot of money and some of us do not. But as different as we may be, we all have one thing that we share — at some moment in time, we lost our confidence in the woman who was inside of us and just needed a piece of encouragement but were to afraid to ask for it.

I have found that when I encountered these moments in my life, I would see or hear a quote from someone that would empower me for that moment of time, sometimes for a minute and other times for several days. That is why I wanted to share these quotes with my fellow sisters as we embark upon life's journey together, empowering one another.

Day 1

If you don't get rid of the
wrong people,
you will never have space
for the right people.

Day 2

You may want success for
someone else,
but they must be willing
to do what is required
for themselves.

Day 3

We may not think the same, but that doesn't mean we don't want the same things.

Day 4

We must learn to work together to accomplish the common goal.

Day 5

Pressing forward during adversity builds character.

Day 6

Successful people
go to work to prosper,
not just to work.

Day 7

Don't lose time living
in regret.
Learn from past mistakes
and move forward.

Day 8

When you are wrong,
admit it.
When you are right,
be quiet.

Day 9

Stop asking God to Bless what you are not committed to.

Day 10

When prayer becomes a habit, miracles become the norm.

Day 11

Don't become so
consumed with what you
are praying for
that you forget to be
thankful for what
you have.

Day 12

Your destiny
is designed for you.

Day 13

The basis of trust
in a relationship is
authenticity,
not perfection.

Day 14

Don't measure
your happiness by
someone else's
standard.

Day 15

Today I choose to stop focusing on what I perceive to be wrong with others.

Today I choose to focus on me.

Day 16

Sometimes we cannot move forward because we can't find total agreement within ourselves.

Day 17

When you allow
God's Word to narrate
the scenes of your life,
then you will know for
certain what must be
done.

Day 18

Healthy relationships
add balance to your life.

Day 19

You cannot put
God and man first
at the same time.

Day 20

When a person says
to you,

"I'm still trying to decide,"

that's their way of saying,

"Not now."

Day 21

Stop loaning people your time; there is no repayment on it.

Day 22

Obedience creates
opportunity.

Day 23

Every new day
is a day to improve
upon yesterday.

Day 24

I'm not perfect.
I do not always make
the right choices.
I do not always have
the right answers.

But I am kept by a God
Who is perfect,
a God Who loves me
despite my choices,
a God Who will correct
my answers.

Day 25

Do not
let anyone else define
your determination,
your drive, your gut,
or your motivation.

Day 26

On the inside of you
is a voice
that will propel you
to the next level.

It is up to you to
decide if you will listen
to this voice or not.

Day 27

You will gain
knowledge and strength
when you are in the
right environment.

Day 28

While I am not
in total control of
what happens in my life,
I am in total control
of how I respond.

Day 29

Only you can create
the place of peace
in your life that allows
you the freedom of
heavenly places.

Day 30

Internal forces
have a greater impact
on your destiny than
external forces.

Day 31

I must suffer
one of two things:

the pain of discipline
today or the pain of
regret tomorrow.

Day 32

God's plan
cannot be given to
someone who has their
own plan in mind.

Day 33

Good intentions
are purely good will
that was intended
to happen
but never did.

Day 34

The harder you work,
the harder it is to quit.

Day 35

Life is like a tire:

As it serves its purpose,
it will endure bumps,
bruises, and potholes
along the way.

Day 36

Your attitude toward wealth and business can cost you millions or make you millions.

Day 37

Sometimes
the smallest things
make the biggest
differences.

Day 38

Goals in action
can move you
from ordinary to
extraordinary.

Day 39

Forgiveness
removes the desire
to get even.

Day 40

To endure is to
continue something
even though there
is confusion,
discouragement, and fear
along the way.

Day 41

Do not give regret control over your future.

Day 42

Only you know
how badly you want it.
So only you know
how hard you must
work to get it.

Day 43

If you don't know
where you are going,
chances are you
will end up in a place you
don't want to be.

Day 44

To be successful,
recognize when to put
your own needs first.

Day 45

Your thoughts have
the power to change
your direction.

Day 46

How long are you
going to play it safe by
sticking with what
you know?

Day 47

Old ways cannot open
new doors.

Day 48

Sometimes
we become better
by helping others
bring out the best
in themselves.

Day 49

Stop
chasing people
who do not want
to be caught.

Day 50

Do not allow
bitterness and envy
to block you from
your Blessings.

Day 51

It is so tempting
to value things that
have no value at all
only to later discover
that you overlooked the
true treasure.

Day 52

Be careful not to
give up opportunity by
settling for familiarity.

Day 53

We all have obstacles
between us
and what we desire.

The question is,
are you willing to do
what must be done
to eliminate the
obstacles?

Day 54

Why start if you don't plan to finish?

Day 55

People too insecure
to follow their own
dreams will always try
to discourage you
from following yours.

Day 56

Do not
discount yourself.
Always remember
your value.

When you forget it,
you give others
permission to do
the same.

Day 57

In the moments of
your greatest struggles,
when your character
is being tested,
don't give up.

Day 58

No one has the right
to control your actions
or tell you how you are
supposed to feel.

Day 59

God knows where I am,
and He can get me where
I am supposed to be.

Day 60

People will buy into me
if I buy into myself.

Day 61

Act, dress, talk, and
walk in the direction
you want to go.

Day 62

To commit to a decision
that is life changing,
I must be willing to be
"all in."

Day 63

Active faith is
staying committed to
your destiny through all
seasons of your life.

Day 64

A life's legacy is built
from individual choices
and decisions.

Day 65

It is better to walk alone with purpose than to walk with thousands and have no direction.

Day 66

Let your *"Yes"* be *"Yes"* and your *"No"* be *"No."*

It's that simple.

Day 67

To be accepted
and liked by others,
you must first accept
and like yourself.

Day 68

If you soar above
your circumstances,
you will be able to look
down and see a clear
pathway.

Day 69

The difference between
who you are and
who you want to be
is what you do.

Day 70

Successful people don't play the blame game.

Day 71

Do not lose yourself
trying to be
what everyone else
wants you to be.

Day 72

If you only focus on
your mistakes, you
will miss the learning
opportunities.

Day 73

Love is innocent.
Love does no harm.
Love forgives.
Love develops.
Love believes.
Love supports.
Love encourages.
Love respects.
Love honors.
Love heals.

So, ask yourself,
is this really love?

Day 74

The level of respect
you have for yourself
is the highest level
of respect you will be
able to receive
from others.

Day 75

Do not compromise your purpose for someone else's purpose.

Day 76

We all get sidetracked.

That doesn't mean you should stop or give up.

It simply means pick up from where you left off and continue your journey.

Day 77

There is power in
your thoughts.

Day 78

A closed mind creates
barriers to growth.

Day 79

When you feel
like stopping, remember
how much you have
accomplished.

Day 80

A sign of wise leadership
is thinking before
speaking.

Day 81

In 20 years,
you will be more
disappointed by the
things you didn't do
than the things
you did.

Day 82

The challenges of life
suggest God's level of
confidence in me.

Day 83

Do not allow your job title to define you.

When you work to your greatest potential,
you have the power to define your job title.

Day 84

Consistency
determines how soon.

The lack of consistency
determines how long.

Day 85

Your life can go one
of two ways — get
satisfaction from the
fruits of your labor or
regrets because you didn't
labor long enough.

Day 86

Love has a way of
unlocking the mystery of
the human heart.

Day 87

You must be willing
to give up good to go
for great.

But to give up good
for great means
there may be a period
when you feel like
you have neither.

Day 88

A broken heart can be healed and restored, which creates opportunities for new beginnings.

Day 89

Your vision doesn't
have to make sense, you
just have to believe.

Day 90

You never know
how close you are to
victory.

Don't stop.

Day 91

Relationships should not
be based on promises
but on commitment
and trust.

Day 92

The only thing wrong
with your dream
is you are resisting
support.

Day 93

To love
requires having enough
faith to let go.

Day 94

Don't let your past
hold you captive.

Day 95

To love people
for who they really are,
you must first love God
for who He really is.

Day 96

Always be
self-improving.

Day 97

Surround yourself
with people who aren't
afraid to see
the greatness in you.

Day 98

Not every relationship
is meant to be.

Day 99

Don't compromise
your passion.

Day 100

Information
received is no good
until you intentionally
put it into action.

Day 101

All great visions
require execution to
become a reality.

Day 102

Success is a series
of failures followed by
a series of victories
fueled by determination
to not quit.

Day 103

Look again — the first impression is not always the correct impression.

Day 104

Daily disciplines
done intentionally make
the difference.

Day 105

Every step
you take toward your
goal is one less step
you will need to take to
accomplish the goal.

Day 106

The desire to achieve
must be stronger than
the impulse to quit.

Day 107

It takes faith
to pursue the desires
of your heart.

Day 108

Life is too short to focus on the negatives.

Day 109

Consistency
has a way of building
commitment, dedication,
and determination.

Day 110

If you don't define
success in your life,
then others
will define it for you.

Day 111

Let your future
be created by your goals,
not by your
circumstances.

Day 112

The time to plant
the harvest is before
the need.

Day 113

Manage your thoughts.

Reject and replace wrong thoughts by recognizing and responding to right thoughts.

Day 114

It is not okay to tell our children to try again if we are quick to quit after one try.

Day 115

Hard work and good luck
are a united couple.

Day 116

To retain a Leader
on the team,
they must be given the
opportunity to lead.

Day 117

God's love is greater
than any love you could
ever imagine.

Day 118

When it looks like the odds are against you, don't give up.

To do so is to join the very forces fighting against you.

Day 119

Stop fighting everything you don't like.

Growth isn't always fun, but it is always necessary.

Day 120

If changing
your ways meant you
could be happy the rest
of your life,
would you do it?

Day 121

God cannot Bless
what you do not do.

Never underestimate
the effort of doing.

Day 122

Intimate relationships
are designed to add value,
not decrease it.

Day 123

God looks beyond
where you started to
calculate your end.

Day 124

Just because
you knew someone
in the past doesn't mean
you know them now.

Day 125

Stop
subtracting from
your life what God is
trying to add.

Day 126

Being thankful
allows us to recognize
our blessings.

Day 127

Do not talk about how
bad your situation is
if you are not willing
to let go of something
to change it.

Day 128

If you dream it,
don't be afraid to do it.

Day 129

The fruit of your life is
a direct product of the
seeds you plant.

Day 130

God inhabits the
praises of His people.
This day,
I choose praise.

Day 131

Trials bring patience
and patience brings
maturity.

Day 132

Even the most
effective Leader
must have a team that
is willing to follow.

Day 133

One of the greatest
opportunities in life
is to do something that
you love to do.

Day 134

Faith is not a feeling;
it is a daily decision upon
which you must act.

Day 135

Sometimes
the only thing left to do
is to resolve to make
it happen, then you are
on your way.

Day 136

The purchase price
always comes before
the product.

Day 137

Your daily habits impact your long-term goals.

Day 138

It's okay to try again.

Never let any disbelief or
fear tell you it's not.

Day 139

For every decision in life,
timing is essential.

Day 140

Always remember,
the God Who called
you has the strength
to sustain you.

Always lean on Him.

Day 141

You are responsible for owning your own happiness.

Day 142

When you are certain
about what God has for
your present and future,
the things of
the past won't bother
you anymore.

Day 143

Conquering
the what if's is a step
toward launching your
destiny.

Day 144

If it interrupts
your peace with God,
then it's not in
God's plan for you.

Day 145

A mind at peace is a strong mind.

Day 146

Do not allow
how someone treats you
to become your excuse
to give up.

Let it be
the driving force that
pushes you forward.

Day 147

God is greater than any
struggle you may face.

Day 148

How you began
doesn't have to be
how you end.

Day 149

If a person can lie to you
about the intimate parts
of their life,
don't trust them
with the intimate parts
of your life.

Day 150

To know me
and to know *of* me are
two different things.

Day 151

As a leader,
it is critical to recognize
when to stop doing and
when to start requiring
others to be accountable.

Day 152

When a person
acknowledges your
innermost beauty but
doesn't respect it,
they weren't fully capable
of handling it.

Day 153

When you are secure
with who you are,
then you can celebrate
the victories of others.

Day 154

Don't share your story
too soon.

Day 155

Do not
let someone be so
focused on who you were
that they do not see who
that they do not see who
you have become.

Day 156

When you are confused by what someone is saying, gain clarity through their actions.

Day 157

Sometimes
to find peace, you must
be willing to come out of
your comfort zone.

Day 158

How you act matters.

How you react matters
even more.

Day 159

Everyone faces
crossroads.

The difference is
the direction that is
chosen.

Day 160

The more you love,
the more you expect.

Day 161

You cannot
treat people one way and
then talk about them
another way.

Eventually your words
will be displayed in
your actions.

Day 162

Be aware of people
who want you to conceal
your confidence.

Day 163

When something hurts too badly to talk about it, pray about it so healing can begin.

Day 164

Sometimes to get
what we desire,
we must give up
what we love.

Day 165

The greatest battles
we face are the battles
inside ourselves.

Day 166

Do not
spend so much time
focusing on
what did not happen
that you lose sight of
what did.

Day 167

Your future begins where your past ends.

Day 168

Our actions teach
our children more than
our words ever do.

Day 169

To live the life
you were destined for,
you must walk by faith
every day.

Day 170

You cannot
put a price on the
power of a
peaceful mind.

Day 171

If the love you give
isn't enough,
there's no other gift
you can give that will
ever be enough.

Day 172

Stop compromising
your desires by waiting
for someone else.

Day 173

The familiar can
become a dangerous
place because it does not
require growth.

Day 174

With every prayer
that you pray,
you must be willing to
work to receive
the benefits.

Day 175

Do your best and trust God to do the rest.

Day 176

You are only
as powerful as your
made-up mind.

Day 177

Don't allow your
fears to cause you
to run away from what
you truly want.

Day 178

To answer your critics, you must go down to their level.

Don't answer them.

Day 179

Your vision must be well-defined to pull you forward.

Day 180

It is not just about
getting started,
it is about having
the right information
so you can start
the right way.

Day 181

To be successful at
networking,
you must help others
as others help you.

Day 182

Failure can only
defeat you
if you succumb to
the moment.

Day 183

Do not be afraid
to travel uncharted paths.

Your pathway to
success is different from
everybody else's.

Day 184

Some of the greatest leaders were created during times of adversity.

Day 185

I challenge you
to quit remembering
what God has already
forgotten.

It is time to forgive
yourself.

Day 186

Don't let
how you started
be your excuse to not
pursue more.

Day 187

Looking at your
life from God's point
of view will expand
your perspective and
thought process.

Day 188

I do not want
to be remembered as
the one who had
so much potential,
but rather
as the one who
tried everything until
they succeeded.

Day 189

The fire isn't meant
to consume us;
it is meant to refine us.

Day 190

Rejection is God's way
of re-routing.

Day 191

You cannot make it happen
by just talking about it
or thinking about it.
You must believe to
make it happen. You must
dream to make it happen.
You must meditate to make
it happen. You must work
to make it happen.
But most importantly,
you must change
to make it happen.

Day 192

It doesn't
cost anything
to dream big,
but it may
cost everything
to not dream at all.

Day 193

Stop looking
around and look
inside yourself to find
the fight to pursue
your dreams.

Day 194

God reserves the right
to remove us
when we allow our plans
to interrupt His work.

Day 195

Sometimes life's most valuable lessons come from life's darkest moments.

Day 196

If my actions today make a positive influence in the life of someone else, then I pray my actions will do the same tomorrow.

Day 197

Decisions
help us start.

Discipline
helps us finish.

Day 198

Do one thing every day
that helps you walk
into your future.

Day 199

Love and hate
are two of the most
powerful emotions.

You decide
which one wins.

Day 200

Until God
is enough for you,
nothing else will ever
be enough.

Day 201

God doesn't look
at your past to qualify
your future.

Day 202

Before asking God
to do something,
make sure you are
willing to do what
is required.

Day 203

Anybody or anything
that tries to pull
you down is already
beneath you.

Day 204

We cannot expect people
to do better until they
know better.

Day 205

If everyone in your
circle is depending on
you for everything,
you are in the
wrong circle.

Day 206

If you focus
too much on being
who or what someone
else needs you to be,
you run the risk of losing
who you truly are.

Day 207

If you don't trust yourself, you will never be able to trust someone else.

Day 208

Part of being strong
is not allowing pain
to convince you
not to try.

Day 209

To obtain victory,
don't give up when
things get hard.

Day 210

Before you seek advice
from someone,
evaluate where
they are in that area
of their life.

Day 211

Your behavior
will tell a corporation
more about your
professional skills
than your portfolio
ever could.

Day 212

If you continue to compare your glass to someone else's, your glass will continue to appear half empty.

Day 213

You cannot burn out
if you were never on fire.

Day 214

Faith cannot fix
what we are not willing
to face.

Day 215

One of the greatest gifts in life is Happiness.

Be a part of sharing in that gift.

Day 216

Self-improvement
and growth should be
both professional
and personal;
one cannot survive
without the other.

Day 217

It is not possible
to praise and complain
at the same time.

Day 218

The greatest way
to ensure customer
satisfaction is to
promote employee
appreciation.

Day 219

You know a person
has changed when they
are willing to meet you
where you are.

Day 220

There are some things you have to forget so that your heart does not keep breaking.

Day 221

As a leader,
you show a level of
respect to your leadership
by who you bring into
positions of elevation
with you.

Day 222

Just as it takes a team to
support your dream,
it takes a team to
support your *why*.

Day 223

If what you want
doesn't line up with
where you want
to go in life,
succumb to the pull
of where
you want to go.

Day 224

If you keep pushing
people away, they may
not come back.

Day 225

What you do with
hardships determines
how your life ends up.

Day 226

I do not want to show up physically but still be missing mentally.

Day 227

Learn to challenge
your fears.

Day 228

The victories in our lives
are our testimonies.

Day 229

Sometimes we give up
because we do not
fully understand the joy
that is before us.

Day 230

Adaptability can be
either your greatest
strength or your
greatest weakness.

Day 231

It takes courage to be vulnerable.

Day 232

There is power in perception.

Day 233

We should not
expect God to do more
on our behalf
than we are willing to
do for ourselves.

Day 234

Do not stop at the point of transition.

You must cross over to receive your change.

Day 235

Our greatest struggles require our greatest efforts.

Day 236

Sometimes it
takes more courage
to walk away
than it takes to stay.

Day 237

Nothing great can
be achieved without
determination, effort,
grind, and grit.

Day 238

I can because they said
I couldn't.

Day 239

Sometimes
the answer to our
question is looking at us
in the mirror.

Day 240

I cannot allow
your opinion of me
to dictate my confidence
in who I know I am
becoming.

Day 241

You might feel
someone else has
changed,
but it may be that
you've changed.

Day 242

Your greatest self
is inside of your own
imagination.

Day 243

My mistakes are not worse than anyone else's. It's just that I know all the details of them.

Day 244

I respect me and
everything about me;
who I was, who I am, and
who I am becoming.

Day 245

The challenges
in my life represent
my level of confidence
in God.

Day 246

Once I knew better,
I wanted better.

Day 247

Part of being a great leader is recognizing the impact your decisions have on others.

Day 248

Faith can see and
hear things that are not
common to the natural
eye and ear.

Day 249

I am here today
because when my mind
said *"No,"*
my faith said *"Yes."*

Day 250

If you are not willing
to commit and work
daily, then your tomorrow
will mirror your today.

Day 251

My actions reflect my
confidence.

Day 252

We succumb to
or overcome challenges
based on our faith
or lack thereof.

Day 253

Faith is action.

Faith can climb mountains and walk through valleys.

Faith requires forward thinking.

Day 254

I will not give up
when others speak
against me.

Their comments
help fuel my
determination.

Day 255

Never underestimate the power of human connection.

Day 256

No matter how
talented you are,
you cannot accomplish
all your goals
without the help of
another human being.

Day 257

When I looked
at my situation, I laughed
because I realized it
hadn't seen my vision.

Day 258

One of the
most powerful lessons
in life is to learn
what not to do.

Day 259

For us to grow as
individuals,
we must learn to
work harder on ourselves
than we do on others.

Day 260

Someone somewhere
is looking at your level of
confidence and feeling
inspired.

Day 261

Every decision
requires an action.

Day 262

The challenges of life are what create the changes in life.

Day 263

People see your life
through your actions.

Day 264

Empathy builds trust.

Day 265

When we listen to what
people are saying,
it eliminates room for
assumptions.

Day 266

Emotional intelligence
is the strength to control
our emotions.

Day 267

In the midst
of a stressful situation,
remember it is not all
about you.

We never know
what someone else is
going through.

Day 268

When life brings
adversity, choose
to be strong.

Day 269

The misfortunes
of life nudge us
so we may discover
our wings.

Day 270

Refuse to linger
on past difficulties.

Commit to overcoming
future ones.

Day 271

A lack of trust destroys foundations.

Day 272

To lead, one must be perceived as worthy.

Day 273

You are the author of
your own story.

Day 274

Don't get so caught up
in making plans for your
life that you forget to live
your life.

Day 275

Stop listening to people
who are not committed
to their own goals.

Day 276

God Blesses us
to win so we can
Bless others.

Day 277

Commitment
helps you to overcome
adversity.

Day 278

Success may look
different than what
you expect.

Day 279

The work required is not always hard.

Day 280

There is more than
enough God for any need
in my life.

Day 281

You must be willing to give up your definition of who you think you are to become who God has destined you to be.

Day 282

If you hold onto
your talents, you are not
making them available
for God's use.

Day 283

The loudest voices are sometimes the most uninformed.

Day 284

To achieve your dreams,
you have to deal with
the very thing you are
running away from.

Day 285

People will talk about you. That is not the problem.

The problem is if you begin to believe what they say.

Day 286

Faith can heal
and direct your life.

Day 287

Little Goal or Big Goal,
both are better than
no goals.

Day 288

Sometimes
what we have in mind is
not what God has
in mind.

Day 289

God uses our disappointments for our strength and protection.

Day 290

Faith is not
the absence of doubt,
it is the means to
overcome it.

Day 291

If God gave us proof
of His promises,
we wouldn't need faith.

Day 292

Sometimes what is happening on the surface is not the real thing.

Day 293

It comes into
your Spirit before it
comes into your life.

Day 294

Desire must be purged in
the fire of prayer.

Day 295

Winning and losing have nothing to do with your circumstances and everything to do with your choices.

Day 296

You can miss
the target by focusing
on plan B
before completing
plan A.

Day 297

In order to win,
you must first believe
that there are no winners
other than you.

Day 298

Our choices
make us who we are.

Day 299

Leaders
create Leaders.

Day 300

Don't allow a moment
of insecurity to keep you
from your destiny.

Day 301

Successful people exercise incredible drive; they keep doing the hard thing long after others are only doing the comfortable thing.

Day 302

Failure isn't fatal;
the failure to try is.

Day 303

There is going to be a point when you have to decide whether to fight or to quit.

Day 304

There is a fine line between making excuses and making progress.

Day 305

Standing with a team, a Leader can conquer worlds.

Day 306

Be the best you
that you can be.

Day 307

Change is a mindset.

Day 308

If you can maintain what you are currently doing, then it only makes sense to see what else you can accomplish.

Day 309

A long-term perspective requires short-term focus.

Day 310

It is the very things that we cannot see or touch that often make the difference.

Day 311

When we allow room for self-improvement, we make room for success.

Day 312

You cannot
change your life
unless you are willing
to change yourself.

Day 313

Freedom
is on the other side of
your fears.

Day 314

You were not
born a winner or a loser;
you were born a chooser.

Day 315

Give it all you've got.
It's not easy, but it is
doable.

Day 316

You will win
with your heart.

Day 317

There is no obstacle
that cannot be
overcome on the road
to Great Purpose.

Day 318

Do not let the desire
to be perfect hold you
back from learning.

Day 319

The Greatest Leader knows how to be both a teacher and a student.

Day 320

It's not the information
that makes the difference
but the use of the
information.

Day 321

Once you envision
where you are going,
you'll realize what
you *don't* need.

Day 322

For your life to get better,
you must get better.

Day 323

We all have the
same number of hours
in the day.

It's what we choose
to do with those hours
that separate us
from others.

Day 324

The road to success appears simple to those who are watching someone else as they travel it.

Day 325

Everything starts
with a choice.

Day 326

Do not be afraid
to take the necessary
actions today
to create the results you
will want tomorrow.

Day 327

Stop wanting
everything right now.

Recognize the power
of patience.

Day 328

Be aware of your thoughts. They will either undermine or support your success.

Day 329

Your happiness
determines your actions
and your actions
determine your success.

Day 330

You must first be able
to keep a commitment
to yourself before
you are able to keep a
commitment to
someone else.

Day 331

Every moment is an opportunity to make a dream come true.

Day 332

Opportunities of a lifetime must be seized during the lifetime of the opportunity.

Day 333

When your mind
and emotions agree, it is
easier to take action.

Day 334

To take control
of your life,
you must take control
of your mindset.

Day 335

When we offer all that we have, freely and without reservation, God keeps track.

Day 336

If you don't
discipline yourself to
obtain your dream,
then someone else will
discipline you to help
build their dreams.

Day 337

The difference
between commitment
and interest determines
the outcome.

Commitment is at
all times.

Interest is when it is
convenient.

Day 338

Maintain positive focus no matter what is going on.

Day 339

Do not become
so image conscious that
you are afraid to fight for
your success.

Day 340

The fact that we are grown doesn't mean we stop growing.

Growing up is automatic, but growth is intentional.

Day 341

Obstacles come our way
to see how badly we
want our goals.

Day 342

To not make a decision *is* a decision.

Day 343

God is more
interested in our growth
than our comfort
because true growth
leads to comfort.

Day 344

It's not the hours
in the work day, it's the
work in the hours.

Day 345

Failure is a slow,
gradual choice that backs
you into a corner.

Day 346

Be quick to break habits
that can break you and
quick to embrace habits
that can build you.

Day 347

Confidence and competence will attract the right people.

Day 348

Sometimes
you have to look back
to move forward.

Day 349

Learn to work hard in silence and let success make the noise.

Day 350

Now is the time to move forward.

Day 351

Adventures require us to use our energy, love, and passion.

Day 352

Every decision you make is an opportunity for change.

Day 353

Only a fool
becomes aware of the
need to change and
doesn't try to change.

Day 354

Stop looking at what
others possess and
look at what God has
given you.

Day 355

Giving is evidence
that you have conquered
greed.

Day 356

All good things in life are
a form of harvest.

Day 357

Don't let your emotions
stop you.

Day 358

Do not let
the judgments of others
stop you from pursuing
your dreams.

Day 359

I should
invest my time and effort
in the things that
give back to me.

Day 360

Always
look for evidence of a
person's expertise before
accepting their advice.

Day 361

I must be willing to
change for my life
to line up with where
I am going.

Day 362

The greatest gift we can give a broken heart is unconditional love.

Day 363

To get where you've
never been,
you must travel a
different path.

Day 364

To make a change, you
have to do it.

Others cannot do it
for you.

Day 365

God says,
"Open your hands to
release the things you
have been holding onto,
so that you are positioned
to receive the overflow
I have stored up for you."

ABOUT THE AUTHOR

Michelle Neely Stowe believes everyone she comes in contact with should leave the encounter with her feeling special. Michelle has the uncanny ability to make every person feel special.

Michelle has an entrepreneurial Spirit and has tried her wings at many things. She is the owner of Michelle Ink, LLC (publishing company) and of Party With US (event planning company).

In her local area, Michelle has touched many lives and her dream is to extend this touch as far as the love will continue to flow. Michelle has a love and appreciation for mankind that you will feel in her writing, you will hear in her voice, and you will see in her smile and in her walk.